D0432980

FEAST DAYS

BY THE SAME AUTHOR

The hoop
Common Knowledge

FEAST DAYS

JOHN BURNSIDE

.

Secker & Warburg
POETRY

First published in Great Britain 1992
by Martin Secker & Warburg Limited
Michelin House, 81 Fulham Road, London SW3 6RB

Copyright © John Burnside 1992
Reprinted 1992, 1994

The author has asserted his moral rights

A CIP catalogue record for this book
is available from the British Library

ISBN 0 436 20103 8

Set in 10/12½ Bembo
Printed in Great Britain by
St Edmundsbury Press Limited,
Bury St Edmunds, Suffolk

a questa tanto picciola vigilia
de' nostri sensi ch'è del rimanente,
non vogliate negar l'esperïenza,
di retro al sol, del mondo sanza gente.

Dante, *Inferno* XXVI

CONTENTS

ACKNOWLEDGEMENTS

Acknowledgements are due to the following:

Observer, PN Review, Poetry Durham, Poetry Review, Verse

SEPTUAGESIMA

'Nombres.
Están sobre la pátina
de las cosas.'
(Jorge Guillén)

I dream of the silence
the day before Adam came
to name the animals,

the gold skins newly dropped
from God's bright fingers, still
implicit with the light.

A day like this, perhaps:
a winter whiteness
haunting the creation,

as we are sometimes
haunted by the space
we fill, or by the forms

we might have known
before the names,
beyond the gloss of things.

OLD-FASHIONED PINKS

The history dies in things
but you keep in mind the endless
mystery of seeds and labels,

and summer is something else besides
the first carnations:
the space between the flowers and the names,

the crematoria and long-demolished
houses, with their Sacred Hearts
and aspidistras,

and rooms above the business of the garden,
their smell of sunburned skin and olive oil,
and once, before you knew to look away,
the sweetened shadows of mortality.

APHASIA IN CHILDHOOD

I

A room in a village schoolhouse: sprinklings of chalk and rice; wingbeats smoothing the windows under a fall of copper-leaf and prayer. Certain constants: quadratic equations; the word in Latin for table. Science in one book; history in the other.

The questions I asked all the time, but never aloud: where is the soul? what does it most resemble? I had an image of something transparent, a fine yet indestructible tissue of buttermilk or chitin. But nobody knew: there was only the sugar-and-clove-scented room, and the mail van passing through, dusted with pollen and ozone, bearing the witness of farmyards and distant towns, and they were *real*.

II

The evidence of home: hairs in the paintwork; broken fingernails between the carpet and the skirting-board. Traces; fibres; the smell of rubber gloves.

In the evening, with friends at the table, we spoke in anecdotes: the red stain of a haunting; a child in a nightdress; a picture of malice: sure-footed, graceful, walking around us on tiptoe. Mere entertainments, which no one would stop to believe.

Yet why repeat these histories if not for the peculiar sound of the victim? For the stoat in the soul: its pink-eyed wonder, its wistful desire for blood?

III

A shoebox of a life: gulls' eggs and bullets wrapped in the sweetness of Wills Whiffs; foxed snapshots of the classroom beauty, smiling at nothing, flirting across the years.

IV

It was always autumn. Each evening the village melted: steeples and slate roofs dissolving in sunset; willows and cedars plunging into dusk. I sat for hours in the radio's dusted warmth. I slept for months. By morning the gardens had reappeared; the fences smoked for miles in the gold suburbs; the hedges filled with water and jewelled birds.

I had lived so long. Maybe minutes. They sent me to school in a raincoat and colourless gloves.

V

Perfection arrives for the pleached hedges and the cress beds in frozen squares below the embankment. The parish map returns: steeples as landmarks; the old bounds of footpath and stream.

I am travelling a country of windows: a whiteness pressed to the glass as if the train was wrapped in iced velvet; the stations distilled to a glitter of frosted stone.

Memory clears: a series of lakes on maps, barely imagined, shrouded in oakwoods and moss.

VI

It keeps getting bigger. Everything points away from where I stand: new alleys scooped from light; street-names and waterglass hedges; paradigms for cherry tree and snow. That one day I spent in the woods, digging leaf-mould: I kept finding thin silvery threads of mildew that dissolved in the air, and I was sure, if I dug a few inches deeper, I would find a being which resembled me in every way, except that it would be white and etiolated, like a finger of bindweed growing under stone.

HOLYLAND

As childhood persists,
like Palestine:
wine-coloured maps,
pages of fish-scale and vellum,

or like an exercise
in mathematics:
the tossed stone
and spreading ripples,

there is something I must calculate
or parse,
a simple equation,
a sentence, constructed of time

and words that no longer
mean what they said,
like *species*, or *spirogyra*.

LOST

The wood where I was gone
for ages, on those Sunday afternoons:

lost on purpose, looking for the lithe
weasel in the grass,

stopped in my tracks, the way you stop
for echoes. Gone into the cool

of summer, passing the line
where sunlight snagged in the nettles,

I wanted the pink-toothed
killer, the casual

expert, the tribal memory of one
who slips into the chicken runs of mind

and works his way with something of my own
bright rage towards the folly of the damned.

COW PARSLEY

That was another country
where anything might be
concealed: frog-chill or adder,
blisters of golden spawn.

A spiderling domain where shade
thickened and settled,
and we ran barefoot into dreams
of lime and cuckoo-spit.

We took it to contain
a foreignness: the undergrowth of forms
we chose to fear,

black fingertips and wings, rust-printed nails
and crouching versions of our secret selves
beneath the froth, all knowing looks and smiles.

AEAEA

To waken there again
behind a veil of silt and linnet bones,
tasting the same pig soul, the same sour tongue;

to trace a palace wall
through viper's grass and vines
in search of home,

which must be far away
since here is strange:
amber bedrooms, webs of blood and moss,

a house of looms where nobody can tell
if love is skill
or fear of being lost.

PENELOPE

The suitors have been and gone. The loom is still. Perhaps he stayed away; perhaps he died.

But now the boy has met an old man on the beach. Even the dog is fooled. She takes him in.

After a time, she becomes accustomed to his voice. He makes her laugh.

And the stories – she loves them for the women. Her other selves: Calypso, Nausicaa.

Every night she lies with him to listen.

Even though she knows they are untrue.

There was nothing to touch. The smell of daybreak
tinted with frankincense; the feel of an empty sheet and
something slipped away; a moment's unidentified black-
ness receding among shadows. She waited. After some
time there were cries and threats, memorised wounds,
the taking of depositions. They spoke of flesh, they
gathered with the dead, but she remained in the cool
garden, trying to place the voice that had gone before her
to the still centre of the shade, fixing in her mind the
sound like poured water and the black footprints rising
through gravel; a hint, perhaps, or only a supposition;
nothing you would mistake for resurrection.

NE DE CEST AN

You know this country: jadis et naguère;
wet treadmarks in the snow; wet crumbled bones;
wet earthworks in the press beneath the stair;
blown plovers' eggs and broken staddlestones.

November. You are sweeping out dead flies
and only notice when the floor is clean
how tidy space appears when something dies
and leaves no mark to show that it has been;

how tidy the inhabitable house
that holds no spectral afterprint in time,
no cold familiar, damp with blood and loss,
only a thread of wind, the clock's neat chime
and common daylight, clear enough to show
what melts and what remains of last year's snow.

WOMEN

I had no way of knowing
what happened under the sea
but for the stories they told
of mermaids who slipped their skins
and came into the human

dark. They died for love;
but this is how everything works,
faery gardens silted in the mind,
undrinkable liquors glinting on the shelves
in basements, wrapped in verdigris

and salt. And women are moving still
in the rooms of the sea,
perhaps of their own volition, perhaps with the tide,
while I stand on the shore with a rolled skin in my hands,
repeating the spell and digging a hole in the shadows.

FLITTING

The feel of the maze
when I sleep in the afternoon
then wake a moment
in the house we left:
the furniture stacked in the van
and her going one last time
from room to room,
as if something had been
mislaid among the crates
and shrouded mirrors.
I hear us calling her still
till she comes to the door
in her raincoat and wine-coloured gloves,
like the girl in the school-book myth
who had known her way,
losing the thread at last, tired and surprised,
with nothing to keep her,
turning away from the silence.

SICK ROOM

She would wake in the early day,
the lamp on her table
burning the dust for hours before I rose,

not reading, or thinking, but going out again
from the dark of her father's house to where
a greeny light was seeping through the woods,

amazed at that perfect answer to the youth
she carried: soft, small rain,

and mushrooms, too sudden and white
to last, though they grew from nothing, like the soul.

As if I could find her again:
an afterprint on the cool
of the towpath at evening,
the ghost of another form
becoming a gap in the moment: what stays behind
when something live has slipped into the dark
inland of a wood, the end of sound
made presence when the churchbells stop
at noon. That nothing can be lost
is false. Some things are lost.
I feel them slip away: almost enjoy
the loosened grip. The space of what is gone.

GOING TO CROSSHILL

We landmarked that road with the silent:
the convent, the school for the deaf,
the lime trees that stood through years
gathering rains, outwearing sleeves of frost,

past where the meadows reached
for a sunrise scarlet and gold
as the flame of the Sacred Heart
on our grandmother's wall.

Remember the morning we stopped
at the holy well,
the dropped coins disappearing in the sand
like fallen souls,

and when we went to kiss her our goodbyes
that weekday evening, in the emptied room,
the silence afterwards that swallowed all
and promised nothing but the dark road home.

On some days, when the snow
falls back and forth,

touching the earth then drifting out again
to icy space;

those days of unofficial
Christmas: birds with rings

and pear trees filled
with eucharistic fruit,

I think of her again, a shape
that melts before it settles

in the mind, yet still suggests
a distance nobody could reach:

gardens that were close
a moment since,

become the islands of an inland sea,
a brilliance, absolute and undefined,

where storms rage
and are silent.

GRANDMOTHER

The wet moonlight on your road
and alchemilla pearled with morning rain
in your straight garden.

I imagine the route you take
is the route you know,
what little there is: the baker's van, the wood,

the anger or regret that waits for years
to show, then rises like a bright
salmon, true at last
to what you are:

a done life put away, something outworn,
laid amongst old linen like a lost
map of ways you never chose to mend
and private gardens no one else could find.

URPHÄNOMEN

I

Sunday; the word in Greek for transmigration; missals of feast days in scarlet ink: Laetere, Rogation, Quasimodo. All afternoon it was morning in America: quiet water falling on the Lakes, fog in the redwoods, the gold leaf of sunlight on Salem and Mariposa. I did my homework in the kitchen, memorizing the sub-families of Liliaceae and the Latin subjunctives, drawing frogs and Cocos seeds, becoming the dusk by degrees as it seeped through the twigs and streetlamps on Fulford Road, a grey I assigned to the soul in scripture books, the sly persistence of a non-existent world, filling my daydreams with old-fashioned tinsel and crime.

II

I think too long about the road and it disappears in a shimmer of fernleaves and headlamps. In the soft hiss of the terminus a fat girl is practising dance steps by the light of the Budweiser sign; another girl asks for 50c and I give her a dollar. Between stops the road recurs, like the wind, or radio waves. I read about those who have vanished: *she drove to the store for some beer; he stopped on the way for a magazine* – I think too long about the road: that taste of the possible, half diesel, half amyl nitrate. Every night I go home in the lilac rain; every morning I go to work, but I always think of walking away, to the absolute motionless summer of inexistence.

III

Discontent. Somewhat like waking at dawn to the gaze
of a faithful and slightly repulsive pet, or how the kitchen
fills with slugs on summer nights, scaling the wall like
the mind on a notion of God. At night I stand at the door
to listen: those soft low sounds, the shifts of negotiation.
A memory of school: the children hung in dust like old
games kit, discarded love letters folded between the
pages of grammar, the aftertaste of incense seeping
through the floor, binding the colourless dead in legions
on my tongue. It is always a weekday evening: small rain
silvers the bounds of laurel; rumpled aertex and mud
commemorate the mystery of pain, the victim wrapped
in smoke and mud, clutching at straws, fingering the girl
beneath the skin.

IV

I wake again in the flat dark: that country of mock-Tudor
houses and road signs with numbers, a blackness I think I
could split open like a pod and find life glittering inside
like a new seed; a life that is shiny and hard, where
someone has gone before, tending the bounds, tapping
out signals in morse code through stair rods and water.

V

This illusion is performed in brilliant sunshine. The street
is empty, the houses are silent, if I am very still I can feel
everything moving a little further apart: Iceland is
drifting away on the cold sea, the cat on the red brick wall
recedes from where I stand, in the middle of the lawn,
like a character left over from a fifties film. Somewhere
inside the house, in an old medicine bottle, or pressed
between the pages of the family bible, a thread of
seaweed or a single petal of frangipani is drying through
years of late shows and annual statistics: the only
evidence of my crime. It will never be found, and even if
it were, no one would know what it meant; though later a
memory will form in my skin like a tumour: a quiet,
untenable life surfacing through coffee and after-shave
when I lock up the house on summer nights, and linger at
the door to taste the distance.

VI

The forensics of railways: mud and water crusting the worn upholstery of the seat opposite; hairline cracks in the paintwork; the bleached skeleta of birch leaves plastered to the window. Out in the woods, a fauna I never see: bottleglass claws and eyes amidst smoke and leaves; frogs and doves; a sub-viral infinity of forms: snowflake, molecule, electron. When I pass through the villages it is always snowing. Sometimes there is music. There must be a way to draw clues from this; it feels like a network of cause and inference, though perhaps it is not a crime that takes place, but a birth, or a parting. All I see are two girls in the playground under the embankment near Gomshall: one holding a torch, the other kneeling beside a low shrub, so that they resemble the figures in Harunobu's print, *Collecting insects by lamplight*. Or another girl runs out from a cottage to wave as the train streams by, and something moves in the window behind her: a dangerous bonelike face I see as I wave back too late, and the girl is replaced by a single oak, set like a crown of thorns in a blanket of freezing fog.

VII

When night comes I know it by feel: the darkness means nothing, what matters is the cool air streaming under the doors, the shivers that run across the room, the sense that, no matter how still it is around the house, there is a movement in the dark that might be an animal of some kind, alive in the wet grass, warm-blooded and so sensitive that each dewdrop on its skin is a needle: if it is alive, it is not innocent, even though it suffers; even though it suffers it is lit with malice, and I feel it, clenched around its breathing, grinning like a weasel in the dark.

VIII

Like one of those peony haiku, the window is open today: a sweetness rises through the watered gravel, sparrows have gathered in the trees and a girl in a blue dress is crossing Shalford Green, so graceful it seems the whole world is moving, and only she is still.

IX

I will sleep as I slept before, but something will be awake
in the room: a part of myself reflected in the cold and the
darkness, and something I do not resemble, which
nevertheless fits me precisely, a form I have moulded
from what I am not, like a carapace, or a shell. And I will
wake, like one of the taken escaped from a day in faery
lifetimes ago: no one will know who I am but I will think
myself home till I realise that some things I begin I cannot
stop, they discard what has been and assume another life,
where home is the house I imagined and never expected:
a sudden renewal, the pleasure of being lost.

EVERYTHING IS EXPLAINED
BY SOMETHING THAT
HAPPENED IN CHILDHOOD

The mystery years: the sly
beginnings of secret loves,
objects flaring, amber in the dark,
hallowed, like the afterlight of icons.

You have no pictures of the first
instant: of seeing the thrush,
or tasting peaches from the neighbour's tree,

only the moment now, come from the mossed
beech woods, with the dust and water smell
of toadstools on your hands,

to where the furniture is steeped in shade,
neutral and persistent as the sheep
you watched this morning from the early train,
grazing the hillside, far in light and silence.

A TALL STORY

He said he was driving back
when the car stalled on Fulford Road
and silence came out to meet him
like a ghost.

And he thought of himself walking out
in the pre-war dark,
a bucket of blueberries warm
and heavy on his arm.

That's when the owl flew down
and hovered above the stopped
bonnet of the Cambridge, barely touching.

So he said. We never quite believed,
and besides, it was hardly a story: it seems the bird
flickered for one chill instant at the glass
then left him, startled, as the engine turned

and he drove on, along the empty road,
like someone taken in a fairy tale
who breaks the spell and brings a stranger home.

FROG

The prince beneath the skin
has come to rest:
sealed in a cage of bone, he will not rise
for fairy tales or spells.

To think I saw in him
another self:
the changeling I might have been
with luck, or daring.

Now all I notice are his blind
offspring, clogging the pond:
their fat black eyelids closed against the mud
and finding me, the way I look in dreaming.

How morning sometimes works,
unpicking our brighter selves from the wool
tangle of the everyday
the way an archaeologist
picks centuries from dust.

How the wind fingers the blown
tulips and the slack
latch on the window frame,
crusting the yellow wood
with paint-flakes and pollen,

the way it slides towards us with the dawn,
filling the hollow stairwell as we lie
awake, not yet surrendered to the known
pretence, the meagre sanctuary of home.

WINTER HOLIDAYS

What will we see, looking back
on this not-quite life?
How it almost snows
over Christmas, those webs of white
dawning across the hills
and melted by noon,

and how we are almost happy with the lit
glitter of the tree,
the stillness that clings to the window
like moss, and the smell of our own
warm comfort filling the house
on long afternoons

till we turn to the nearly blue
of night on the glass,
or stand out in the garden looking up
at circles of counted stars
and feel ourselves a little strange again,
neutrals in the mystery of presence.

URBAN MYTHS

The secret versions of ourselves,
truthful because they seem
remembered: laughing children
hidden amongst lupins,
cars by the roadside vanishing in fog;

and terrors we meant to avoid
tracking us through a long
acquaintance:
blood on the kitchen floor, blood in the roof;
networks of bone and nerve in drifted leaves

snagging the rake; a perfume of resurrection
filling our throats, sweeter than we expected,
the scent of a garden surrendered to someone else,
the ghosts in its shrubbery only this moment's loss:
a life recalled, that could not happen now,
like summering elms, or the Jesus who walks in carols.

PLEROMA

Smoke from last night's fire above the lawn
and mist in the hedge, a faint
wet visitant;
on mornings such as this, you sometimes find
pure space, like some
entombment in a ritual of birth:
a smoothness cold to the touch
where the garden ends,
the cypress standing in a wave of white
and buried echoes, sounding where you stop
to meet the sun
as if its light were something you had
formed around, a brightness from within,
the life before you are, that always was.

ANAMNESIS

Something I have to remember:
a shopping list for the long-dead,
sizes and shapes of buttons
or fish-hooks and lures,

or the poem, that forms on the lips
and ends on the page,
the way I knew it once, pure glint and slide:
the fat trout in the shade of Fulford bridge,
their fox-eyed nearness
swimming with the tide.

SCHOOLS

I remember the use of the dative,
and calculus, a Roman word for stone,
and how the Romans used a small white stone
to mark the better days.

But you are a different language,
a word they use in the hills
for species that do not appear
in field guides,

a name for the thin,
damp music strangers hear
out walking on the moor,

a pagan grammar scribbled in the dust
when empires fall
and monasteries are lost.

Something has crossed the fields,
a series of claw prints
filling with plum-coloured water;

the stations run for miles:
a single whiteness threaded to the sun;
out in the woods

song-thrushes shiver the snow
from hazels, and the after-stain
of vixen is an echo from the book

of stories children tell on journeys home:
half-disbelieving, fingering the glass,
matching each flake of snow with inward brightness.

DISCIPLINE

The deep morning: how light evolves
through mauves, in the watered
stillness of suburbs,
and how there are always tracks across the lawn
though nothing that could have made them
is visible, only a washed
sunrise filling the hedge
with wings, those disembodied
echoes of a waking at the root
of waking up, and something that resembles
rage, though joyous, in the pure
amazement of a moment that is lost
most surely, being lived as something else.

NOT IDEAS ABOUT THE THING
BUT THE THING ITSELF

I was standing out in the field,
in the first snowfall of winter,
watching the moon scud clouds
like a fat carp drifting through water.
Something had gone before me to the cold
centre of the wood
and I walked after, following a trail
of pawprints that rose through the grass
a step at a time, till it seemed
I was stalking myself towards
some animal brightness hidden in the snow:
a tension; the casual mention in a song
of fox; a given, unrepentant life;
the knowledge of an old reality.

CANTICLE

When it rains
and the garden is cool

and blackbirds return to the wet
borders of our land,

we think ourselves the tenants
of a borrowed house,

with nothing to protect, nothing to claim,
only the moment when singing is resumed

amongst the trees,
and evening fills the grey and green

reflections of the people we reveal
in darkened glass:

the people in a psalm,
firstborn and true,

arriving here by chance,
just passing through.

The pleasures of finity:
autumn; the smell of windfalls;
bundles of letters
from friends we no longer place
quickened on the fire
and gone to dust;
the grease of mirrors,
pure mortality.

And how we imagine the dead
arriving beyond their lives
on nights like this,
as if someone had come to the door
and waited till we went
to open: nothing there;
only the year's first ghosting of new snow
melting as it falls between our windows.

I am lost in a dream
where nobody will come
to find me;
following a path into the frost,
a child again, with numbers in my head,
playing that game of chance:
to call it home
wherever I arrive,

till I wake in the satin dark
clutching at the taste of smoke
and apples,
thinking I am back among the dead
and watching the sudden daylight
bleed across the snow to where I stand,
my fingers on the window
making Christmas.

ETERNAL RETURN

You happen again for a summer,
sit for a snapshot again on a broken wall,
a wave of shadow frozen in the grain
and poppies red again behind your smile.

That was a Thursday in August, in the speed
of youth, and it was Thursday when you died,
flexed against the rhythm of a cold
visitant; reduced to monochrome.

Now I am learning not to dream
in black and white,
watching the gold reappear in a run of shade,
and losing your absence. Learning to let it happen.

GUESSWORK

There was something I should have seen
in those stories of the genie in a stopped
bottle: that fathomed anger
waiting for the innocent to come,
his sweet breath like a memory
of civet, or attar of roses
a thousand years old.

                Sometimes it rained
for days, in the summer break,
a sooty perfume seeping through the house
to where I listened,
and something would stop in the room
where I thought you were working,
as if you had found the bottle of your rage
and paused, with your hand on the stopper
a moment too long.

THE USES OF FOLKSONG

This Samuel Palmer garden, with its
magic apple tree,
inviting a deeper night
than happens in these parts,

this window of burnished landscape,
its birches and homecoming birds,
like one of the uses of folksong, to suggest

a dusk so clear I think it is myself
made distance, where the dead are coming back
through wheat fields and wind-threaded water,
wading towards the echo in my heart.

HEAVEN

That was a place we credited:
a household of constant arrivals
behind a wall of bottleglass and rails,

the country we learned in school
from books that seemed to show us something else,
fishing nets and maps of Ancient Rome.

That one afternoon when it was always
autumn: leaves in the yard,
cats in the upper rooms,

a voice from behind a door calling us in
to sit down, and the sweetness of scones
dissolving the loves we had carried
like stones for so long.

MUERTE A LO LEJOS

Nothing is urgent. The fruit matures and falls
in these gardens around the city
graveyard, where blackbirds feed
on pears and medlars
in the steady autumn rain.

But the day will come when the blackbird
stops; you will be sitting in the warm
kitchen, reading, wrapped in the scent
of lemon or azarole, and that look
will happen: a quiet, unpitying

interest between two rains,
the traffic lost in the streets, the book
face-down to mark your place, space
widening around the kettle's
singing and the bird already gone.

EASTER SATURDAY

A subtler festival:
the light unchanged along a northern street,
the churches locked
on candles and narcissi,
a quick dust
disappearing into gold;

how it rained at the edge
of privet and flowering currants,
or frosted the spilled coal
on back-yard paths,

and yet the red sun stood above the park
in vigil, when communion girls came home
from town, with Easter veils
and laced bouquets,
scrubbed echoes from *The Song of Bernadette*
remembered in a pause between epistles.